PREFACE

"Racism is a pariah, a disease which causes everything in its path to wither and die. It is reality at its ugliest. It sparks unfounded hate, unwanted fear, and promotes unnecessary violence. It disrupts the core principle of *equal justice for all* and unfolds the fabric of American patriotism."

- Robert LeRoy Butler III, M.D.

This book is dedicated to my lovely sister, Dr. Julie Renee Butler

Dr. Julie Butler

Veterinarian who cared for Harlem and its pets

My sister, Dr. Julie Butler, owned and operated the 145th Street Animal Hospital. She lived by the principle, "If you have it to give, you give," caring for animals and opening her home to friends in need.

She earned a doctorate from Cornell University College of Veterinary Medicine, where she was the only African American in her class. Dr. Julie R. Butler took over the 145th Street Animal Hospital on April 1, 1989. For many years it was the only full-service vet clinic in Harlem.

Dr. Butler was deeply committed to caring for animals. From the time she was a little girl, growing up in New Rochelle, N.Y., she knew she wanted to be a veterinarian. Her favorite things about being a vet were performing complex surgeries and serving the African American community. She hired and mentored aspiring veterinarians and technicians. She also co-founded the nonprofit: NY Save Animals in Veterinary Emergency, to provide funds to the owners of pets in need of emergency care.

Even after 30 years, her practice was still a high-wire act. As a sole practitioner, Dr. Butler worked long hours, often getting home well past midnight. Overhead, equipment, and staffing were all increasingly costly.

"She was never really focused on the business side," Dr. Butler's husband, Claude Howard, said. "She was interested in the animals. There were people that swore by her because she saved their pets lives."

On April 4, 2020, Dr. Butler died from complications of the Novel Coronavirus at her home in Harlem. She was 62. She is survived by her husband, son, daughter, and four siblings. She is missed by all.

DEEMED UNWORTHY

BEING A DOCTOR IS NOT ENOUGH

Understanding Racism Through the
Raw Memoirs of a Black Man

ROBERT LEROY BUTLER III, M.D.

ISBN: 9798690055257
Printed in the United States of America

Contents

CHAPTER 1

What is the definition of racism?

rac·ism

Noun

1. Prejudice, discrimination, or antagonism directed against a person or people on the basis of their membership of a particular racial or ethnic group, typically one that is a minority or marginalized.

   Similar meanings: racial discrimination, racialism, racial prejudice, xenophobia, chauvinism, bigotry, bias, intolerance, anti-Semitism, apartheid.

2. The belief that different races possess distinct characteristics, abilities, or qualities, especially so as to distinguish them as inferior or superior to one another.

———— • ————

What is racism and where does it come from? Is it merely an inbred, genetic aberration that subliminally considers white privilege commonplace? Does this, then, provide white people with an underlying, exclusive agenda? Is it socio-politically and socio-economically motivated to keep the so-called *superior* at the pinnacle of power, and the so-called *inferior* subjugated? Is it a socio-psychological formula to control the masses of minorities by keeping them in the dark concerning the true reality of what racism really is? No matter what your reasoning might be concerning racism; it is a cruel and unrelenting way of maintaining control over minorities, by openly and systemically denying them basic civil rights and opportunities on all levels: socially, politically, educationally, and economically.

———— • ————

The 50's and 60's provided a social landscape of racial bias and discrimination. This was a chaotic era that set a backdrop for racial discourse, fear, and anxiety. It was a time when racial unrest fractured the core principles of the American way, putting patriotism on the back burner. Optimism as a nation quickly dwindled into overwhelming despair. The climate of sociopolitical and socioeconomic inequalities bore resentment in both Blacks and whites, which created a dichotomy that significantly impacted dialogue on race relations. This was a time when the federal government reluctantly began to explore and address the overt racism and discrimination, as well as the potential effects it had on the nation as a whole. Brown v. Board of Education, which overturned the "separate but equal" doctrine in Plessy v. Ferguson, prompted the United States Congress to address some of the inequalities, and the systemic racism that had plagued the Black race for centuries.

The Civil Rights Movement paved an unrelenting road in demanding equal justice, not just for Blacks, but for all. The 50's and 60's turned out to be turbulent times: from the

Montgomery Bus Boycott, to the Birmingham Bombings, to the March on Washington…change was demanded. Congress eventually stepped up by enacting two important measures which had initial significance in attempting to bridge the racial divide. The goal was to overturn race-based inequities and to recognize the discriminatory racial imbalances that so greatly plagued the nation. The first was the Civil Rights Act of 1964, which barred discrimination in public facilities and employment. The second was the Voting Rights Act, which was implemented a year after, barring the practices of voter discrimination and the disenfranchising of Black voters. During this time, Martin Luther King—a peace loving Black Leader— was assassinated while working on plans for the Poor People's Campaign in Washington, D.C. and while taking up travel to Memphis, Tennessee to support striking sanitation workers.

——————— • ———————

I was born December 29, 1958 at Mount Vernon Hospital in New York; to Robert LeRoy Butler, Jr and Naomi Bryant Butler. I was named Robert Leroy Butler III. The name was handed down from my grandfather, to my father, and then to me. I am the second oldest of five siblings. My father was born in Greenville, South Carolina and my mother was born in Tallahassee, Florida. They were both highly educated individuals. My father was a brilliant electrical engineer and my mother was valedictorian at Florida A&M *and* a poet laureate.

My father was one of the only officer grade Black men in the Air Force at that time. He had an uncanny love for engineering and his dream was to become an Air Force pilot. I remember him applying, only to be rejected due to the color of his skin.

He eventually served his time and he and my mother ended up migrating to the Bronx, New York in the 50's.

It was an extremely hard existence because of the racial climate during that time. Being Black *beget* an automatic inequality in obtaining both educational and employment opportunities, compared to whites. The unfounded hatred of Black people seemed to cave in on me from all directions, without any logical reason. The thought of being discriminated against, merely because of skin color, was unfathomable to me.

Although my mother was a highly educated woman; she was *still* Black. She was looked down upon as low, inferior, and sub-human. Her intellectual prowess was envied by her white counterparts, yet she was never taken seriously. She experienced door after door repeatedly slammed in her face after every interview she went to, but she had the confidence and innate perseverance to never give up when it came to seeking employment. Both my father and mother were empowered human beings who instilled in us the importance of education, hope, and following our dreams, despite obstacles and overwhelming adversity. My mother took any job she could, at all hours of the day or night to help support the family. She did not complain or reveal an ounce of negativity while doing what she felt she had to do. She was an immensely proud woman. I remember going on a temporary job outing with her. While the white people used the front entrance of the building, we had to enter the building through an alternate door on the side. She *attempted* to explain why we were not treated the same as white people. As repetitive as this theme was throughout my childhood; they were experiences and observations I was too young to comprehend. After all the rejections, my mother eventually landed permanent employment as a business math and accounting teacher at New Rochelle High School in New Rochelle, New York.

My parents were not only good parents, but exceptionally great parents! They fostered a nurturing love filled with compassion, concern, and an unconditional commitment to family that lives with us to this very day.

———— • ————

Living in the projects of New York required constant awareness. This awareness was heightened by the notion that any unknown variable could be a danger to my well-being. I could be harmed or even killed by the establishment; or by the drugs, violence, or crime that was so prevalent on the streets every day. The fear was real, and the reality hit home for my parents. They realized—to properly raise a family—they would have to determine how to climb out of their current socioeconomic existence. With hard work and determination, my parents were able to move us out of the projects in the Bronx, and into a small community in New Rochelle about 20-30 minutes outside of New York City. The move was a step-up demographically and socially, but it was not devoid of social imperfections and racial undertones. We moved into a community of first-and second-generation Irish Catholic and Italian Catholic immigrants. Our acceptance, or lack thereof—being the only black family in the small town—was less than ideal. The language barriers hindered effective communication and the educational level of some of the first-generation immigrants made communication virtually impossible. It was an extremely difficult transition. We were constantly harassed, with bricks repeatedly thrown through our front windows, and loud screams of, "Niggers go home," throughout the days and nights. The most terrifying experiences were waking up multiple times—in the middle of the night—to crosses burning on our front lawn! No human being should have to endure such violent demonstrations of hate, *simply* because of the color of their skin.

Social isolation can produce profound psychological issues and negative responses. It can hamper the development of self-esteem and hinder confidence. This can have grave impacts on any minority population. Social development is also disrupted, which can lead to a negative impact in gaining a proper progression of education which can eventually have strong economic implications.

Our family not only endured an ongoing level of hatred

and social prejudice, which was outright ignored during that unsettling era; we suffered financial hardships as well. There were many times when we did not have enough to eat. Rice and oatmeal— three times a day—was *normal.* Due to lack of finances, the heat and electricity were often shut off by the gas and electric companies for weeks at a time. I have the unpleasant memory of having to boil water, one kettle at a time, to add to a tub filled with frigid water—even during the winter months— to take a bath. Those were harsh and unforgettable times.

———— • ————

I attended Jefferson Elementary school in New Rochelle, New York with my two sisters. We started our days, sometimes with a meal in our bellies, and sometimes not. We walked five miles one way to school, and five miles back home. This was a recurring theme, even during the winter months. I recall many days walking to school in the snow with holes in the soles of my shoes. I often had to line my shoes with plastic bags to avoid experiencing wet feet during class.

My Family

Attending elementary school was not void of its social and racial problems. In the beginning of 3rd grade, my development was stifled due to a speech impediment. It was a wonder that the educational system did not recognize this defect during my previous grades. It was surmised that this was due to my "Negro" heritage and the school administration blamed the speech impediment on culturally genetic causes. My parents and I were told that "Negros" are born with larger tongues than whites and their tongues did not fit in their mouths properly, thus anatomically causing a disruption in speech patterns. This is called, *macroglossia*. Somehow, they coupled this absurd theory to the stigma of mental retardation. Nonetheless, they decided I was considered developmentally delayed and the goal was to place me in a special education curriculum. My mother, being the educator she was, demanded through petition, that I be evaluated by a speech pathologist. It was determined that my intellectual level was that of a 4th grader and that I had a true speech pathology issue. I had difficulty pronouncing glides, fricatives, and diphthongs and after only three weeks of training by the speech pathologist, my speech impediment had resolved. This was a prime example of the bias that was inherent in the school systems.

I remember, while still in elementary school, being reprimanded for standing up to recite the Pledge of Allegiance with my all white class. Black children were not allowed to stand and recite the Pledge of Allegiance, even though, ironically, it was meant to stand for unity and freedom. Every time I stood up; I was punished. I was forced to sit in the coatroom, in the dark, on a dunce chair, with a dunce hat on my head while all the other children played on the playground during recess. There were times when the punishment also included taking away my lunch. The harsh discipline was culturally insensitive, unnecessary, and disproportionate, which created a cumulative effect in diminishing enthusiasm and motivation for learning.

———— • ————

I have fond memories of my parents. My mother was a beautiful, gifted Black woman who was extremely talented in many ways. She was an intellectual, an educator, and a scholar. She was also warm, nurturing, and compassionate. She was able to take any negative burden we were experiencing and turn it into a positive, constructive life lesson. She never showed her feelings concerning the racial plight the nation was going through during that time, maybe, so as not to burden us. Not only was our mother an educator, she was also a disciplinarian. We would come home from school and the first thing we were told to do was to go straight to our room and do our homework. This was prior to dinner *and* there was certainly no time for play. Homework was serious business. This was a hard knock existence. This was no joke. Yes, she was our professor *and* she was our Mom. Looking back, I was fortunate to have parents who pushed the importance of education.

My Dad

My father was an intellectual in his own right. Not only was he a gifted electrical engineer, he was the *Black MacGyver* of his time. MacGyver was based on a TV series that began airing in the 80's. It was based on a character that possessed a genius-level intellect, proficiency in language, superb engineering skills, excellent knowledge of applied physics, military training techniques, and excellent conflict resolution. My father was all this and more. I have many memories working side by side with him doing all kinds of home projects. Whether it was fixing cars, laying carpet, putting up paneling, plumbing, building model cars/airplanes, painting, sanding & staining hardwood floors, repairing transistor radios & tube televisions, landscaping, and the list goes on! My father did it all with the heartfelt nurturing a son needs for proper growth. He was also a disciplinarian. He had a way of letting us know when we did something wrong. At times, he would use switches on us to make sure the message hit home and *stuck*. Thankfully, that type of discipline was infrequent.

Innately, my father knew what being Black in America meant. It meant being psychologically and physically attacked for no reason other than the color of your skin. Being Black also meant not being given the opportunity to work because you were deemed intellectually inferior. Black people were not even allowed to freely hangout in public venues, because it was against the law. Reflecting on the discipline makes me wonder if my parents were being protective and shielding us from societal harm.

———— • ————

I recall, in 1965, when I was only 7 years old, it was advertised that the "Sound of Music" would be playing at the New Rochelle mall theater. I was excited and eager to see the movie, but most importantly to see it with my father. We showed up at the theater, only to have the person at the ticket office say, "Sorry, we don't allow your kind in here." I remember those words distinctly and they will forever be etched in my mind. I was confused and bewildered as to why we were not allowed in the theater to watch the movie. I looked up at my father with tears forming in my eyes and the answer I got was, "They just don't allow our kind in." The hurt that was portrayed through my father's demeanor—as well as the expression on his face—was devastating to witness, especially as my father struggled to give a *valid explanation* regarding the obvious act of racism.

I am still trying to grasp what happened during that incident. I wondered, was it me personally? Was it the way I looked? Was it due to my young age? Was it the way I dressed? Was it because we were not as financially secure as others around us? Did this happen by chance? However, subconsciously, and deep in my heart and soul, I knew it was because of the color of my skin.

———— • ————

What is skin color? According to Wikipedia, "Human skin color: ranges in variety from darkest brown to lightest hues. An individual's skin pigmentation is the result of genetics, being the product of both of the individual's parents' genetic makeup, and exposure to sun. In evolution, skin pigmentation in human beings evolved by the process of natural selection primarily to regulate the amount of ultraviolet radiation penetrating the skin, controlling its biological effects."

The perception of skin color greatly overshadows who a person really is. There is an inherent bias in our society toward favoring lighter skin over darker skin. There is a casual relationship between self-esteem and the contrast levels of skin color. Lighter skinned people are more apt to have higher self-esteem and more positive character traits, influencing more socioeconomic opportunities. The darker skinned person tends to exhibit lower self-esteem and reveal a lack of confidence, which has a direct relationship in fostering unhealthy psychosocial development and inversely less socioeconomic opportunities.

Racism and skin color have a definite effect and inverse relationship in the psychological development of children. Thus, hinders proper adolescent development which seeps into young adulthood and forward into adulthood. It stifles Black people on levels socio-politically, socio-economically, and educationally. The psychological stress of racism and stereotyping, re-enforces victimization which undermines academic performance, disrupts the development of cognitive skills, diminishes problem solving development, slows vocational attainment, and displaces developmental milestones. There is wide disparity and inequality in America's educational system, preventing Black children from realizing their full potential. The lack of educational achievement plays an important role in future socioeconomic outcomes and can impact health as well.

———— • ————

I was in a terrible accident when I was 4-1/2 years old. I was playing in the kitchen at our home in New Rochelle, New York. I often played under the kitchen table while my mother was making breakfast. I would pretend to be different cartoon characters, such as: Deputy Dawg, Fred Flintstone, or Yogi Bear. I would sometimes imagine I was a superhero, like Superman. I could jump over buildings and was faster than a speeding bullet! Those were memorable times. Those were great times. Those were the times when we sat at the breakfast table, as a family, and shared our love and admiration for each other. One of those early mornings—while under the kitchen table—I decided to play hide and seek with one of my sisters. I was the seeker. I closed my eyes and began the pursuit. I heard my sister's voice squeal out with laughter as I got closer and closer to her. I reached out and inadvertently pulled down on the frying pan handle—of a pan filled with hot bacon oil— that was sitting on the stove. The pan landed on the entire left side of my face. I let out a high-pitched shriek. The pain was unimaginable. I felt the skin on my face blister up almost instantaneously. There were even pieces that peeled off as I stood there. First, I was hysterical and then I went into shock. My skin color appeared *ashen*. I became clammy and weak. My lips turned blue and I lost consciousness. My mother was frantic, but she did not panic. She wrapped me in a blanket and rushed me to the local hospital. We arrived at the Emergency Room only to be turned away. We were refused medical care because, "No colored people allowed."

Growing up in New York there were few doctors available to provide healthcare for Black people. We were not allowed into the local hospitals or clinics because of their *white only* designation. We were fortunate, however. My mother remembered that there was a doctor in the community who accepted and cared for Black patients. She was a white pediatrician who practiced out of a solo clinic on the outskirts of New Rochelle. We quickly ventured to the clinic. My mother rushed me in as she held me with love, wrapped in the blanket. The Pediatrician, who appeared to be in her 70's, with a tall stature, and a German accent, escorted my mother and me to one of the examination rooms for assessment. By the time I started to become slightly alert, some of the blisters began to ooze and my face became increasingly red and swollen. My mother was told I had extensive 2nd and 3rd degree burns. The worst news was the burns would leave permanent scarring and disfigurement.

Because of the *white only* designation, we were not allowed entrance into a hospital to see a burn specialist, dermatologist, or surgeon for a skin graft consultation. Even if we had been granted entrance into the hospital for medical care; we did not have the finances to cover the cost of treatment.

My parents could not afford to pay for the clinic visits either, but the doctor never asked for any payment for her services. The Pediatrician provided all medical supplies, medications, and follow-up visits free of charge! She tended to the burns until the left side of my face healed with some scarring. The pain was immense during my healing process and knowing I would be disfigured for the rest of my life was disheartening. Nonetheless, she treated my family with equal fairness and never once turned us away because we were considered societally different and financially incapable. Although it was determined by the pediatrician that my face would be disfigured for life; I miraculously and completely healed with no scarring or disfigurement! This happened over a one-year period after being released from her care. She could not determine any medical reason for my *miracle*.

———— • ————

Even today, skin color has its effect on the availability of proper medical care for Black people; with racism and lack of financial stability being the major contributing factors in preventing proper access to healthcare. Black infant mortality is also higher compared to other countries throughout the world. Although America is one of the wealthiest nations in the world, black men and women experience the highest mortality rates. Systemic racism prevents access to well needed healthcare, which should be universally available to all Americans. Sadly— when it is available—it is difficult to access, of lower quality, and it is not affordable. *Color inferior healthcare* stems from socioeconomic and sociopolitical obstacles inherent in *white America,* which makes it difficult for the Black community to overcome. This is a dilemma. Blacks have a higher rate of diabetes, cardiovascular disease, hypertension, breast cancer, and prostate cancer compared to whites. The lack of access to proper healthcare leads to a disproportionately higher death rate. Black people dying unnecessarily due to inadequate healthcare because of skin color, is a travesty. Preventive care is important in thwarting chronic diseases but the development of culturally adaptive systems—which provide appropriate educational tools to achieve this—is lacking. Disparities in healthcare are culturally biased across the board. The bias is not only seen in America as a whole, but in individual physicians as well. Preconceived racial bias contributes further to the inadequate care Black people receive, which continues the cycle of unnecessary morbidity and early mortality from an unfair healthcare system.

CHAPTER 2

The 70's and 80's were years fraught with persistent inequalities and discrimination. Race-conscious *remedies* came into play to try and assist in equaling the imbalance of racism. This was a time when the first black woman ran for president. Her name was Shirley Chisholm. This was a time when John. F. Kennedy called for the federal government to hire more African Americans, recognizing the disparity in employment opportunities. It was a time when the term "reverse discrimination" was first used: "Discrimination against members of a dominant or majority group, in favor of members of a minority or historically disadvantaged group. Groups may be defined in terms of disability, ethnicity, family status, gender identity, nationality, race, religion, sex, sexual orientation, or other factors." It was also a time when prominent Black civil rights leaders and prominent actors helped redefine and influence the mindset of mainstream America. The bottom line, though, is racism was still a prevalent, negative force in our nation.

Although racism was central and core in hindering change, the picture was much more complicated. One area of importance which racism had an effect on, was education. There was a glaring gap that separated Black people, especially on the level of educational attainment and achievement. Some believed the problem stemmed from the widened gap in family income, single parent families, increased violence in the inner-city environment, and the introduction of crack cocaine and drug related gang wars. The *chaos in the streets* made the classroom environment stressful. The educational deficiencies hit Black children the hardest, yet they were the most in need of education. The outcome of the racial insensitivity concerning the lack of educational equality, immensely affected Black academic performance. There was also a cultural bias inherent in standardized tests which further hindered the Black community and the development of their cognitive skills. The vicious cycle becomes harder and harder to correct, and as a result, creates a lack of proper educational skills for future success. Black students were just pushed through the educational system, which in the end, not only affects education, but employment opportunities compared to white people as well. The climate: with its sociopolitical, socioeconomic, and educational inequalities created resentment in both Blacks and whites, which significantly impacted race relations.

Thus, progress—by many measures seemingly so clear—is viewed as an illusion, the sort of fantasy to which intellectuals are particularly prone. But the ahistorical sense of *nothing gained*, is in itself bad news. Pessimism is a self-fulfilling prophecy. If all our efforts as a nation to resolve the "American dilemma" have been in vain—if we've been spinning our wheels in the rut of ubiquitous and permanent racism, as Derrick Bell, Andrew Hacker, and others argue—then racial equality is a hopeless task, an unattainable ideal. However, if both Blacks and whites understand and celebrate the gains of the past, we will move forward with the optimism, insight, and energy that further progress surely demands.

———— • ————

As a child I felt that being Black was undesirable and identifying oneself as Black was a stigma which created unwanted shame and feelings of disgrace. The subtleties of racism, profiling, and stereotyping creates forced polarization, lack of confidence and a demoralizing sense of nonacceptance simply due to skin color. It is unfair and unjustifiable. Racism is a *metastatic* cancer that continues to spread to this day. How many times must we struggle to be recognized and heard? Why must we put forth such great effort to fight against discrimination? There are many questions like these with no distinct clear answer, but we must acknowledge: discrimination should be universally condemned. Racism has ultimately led to the polarizing concept of white v. Black. To heal we must begin to tear down the distrustful, seemingly immovable racial barriers that have plagued our nation for hundreds of years.

———— • ————

Junior high was a time of unsure transition and anticipatory excitement. I remember my first day of school at Isaac E. Young Junior High School in New Rochelle, New York. My excitement on that day, quickly turned into fear. As I walked into school, I was met with racial slurs and epithets. I remember a small section of West Indian students becoming involved in a scuffle with a group of white students. A loud scream came from one of the white students. The student was stabbed in the chest multiple times. Blood seemed to be coming from all directions! After being stabbed, he was thrown out of the second-floor window! With force, he met the unforgiving concrete below. He was not moving and appeared to not be breathing. My heart rate accelerated, and my chest pounded uncontrollably. That day was the beginning of a race riot. Students were in a frantic rage; punching, fighting, stabbing, scrambling, and running. There was mass confusion and chaos all around! I remember running away and not stopping until I finally reached home. I will never forget that day. It took time for peace to be restored, but eventually the academic year commenced *normally*.

I had an admiration for science and did quite well in those studies. Prior to starting 9th grade, the school offered a test for advanced honor classes in all academic disciplines. This would place a person one year above their current class year. After taking the test for AP Biology, I was completely confident that I would be placed in the advanced class. The day of reckoning came, and the grades were posted. I passed and not only passed, but I scored the highest grade of all the test takers. I was elated! The first day of 9th grade came quickly, and I remember the excitement I had anticipating attending the 10th grade Honors Biology Class. Sadly, I was sorely disappointed when I arrived at the class. I was met with a rather angry, bewildered teacher who demanded I turn around and head to the principal's office.

He expressed; he would not allow people like me to attend his class. Yes, I was the only black student in the class. The class was—and always had been—an all-white environment. My mother quickly petitioned my entrance back into the class. She went through the Board of Education and surprisingly, the decision was in my favor! They deemed the teacher's decision unconstitutional, discriminatory, and a violation of my basic civil rights. I was to be allowed, by congressional mandate, to attend the class. It was not easy for me after I was back in class. I was met with overt intimidation; not allowed, at times, to participate in all the lab practicums; and was often ostracized and excluded socially by my classmates. Although I performed at a high academic level, I was given a final course grade of B-, while my white counterparts all received A's for their effort.

———— • ————

My Mitt

I have always been exceptionally agile; with incredible eye and body coordination skills, amazing physical timing, and the mental and competitive edge to win. You could say, I was gifted in sports. I remember my father returning home from work one day with an expression of glee on his face. He had a special surprise for me. I was uncontrollably antsy and could not wait to discover what he had hidden in the paper bag he was holding. My eyes were fixated as my father reached into the bag. He pulled out a baseball mitt. It was one of the most amazing gifts he had ever given me, because I loved baseball! I remember every day after my father finished a hard day's work, he would take me to the park to coach me. We practiced a myriad of baseball skills, which I became extremely proficient in. My father—proudly knowing how great those skills had become—prompted me to try out, not just for the junior baseball team, but the varsity baseball team! Being a 9th grader and trying out for the varsity team would place me at the high school level of play. I remember the astonished expression on the coach's face as I tried out. My baseball skills, agility, and quickness surprised the coach, as well as the players.

I did not make the cut. The coach said, "Your kind would not make a good fit for the team." He did not want to disrupt the harmony of his team. The caveat was obvious. I did not want to acknowledge the fact that the rejection was due to my skin color and cultural identity. However, there was no escaping reality, this was a discriminatory act which was racially motivated. I was the only black player who tried out for the varsity baseball team and I was rejected. The bottom line, he did not want to accept a person of a different race on his baseball team. It was a devastating blow and a terrible disappointment. This was one of the first times in my young life I felt hopeful of being accepted on talent alone. My confidence, self-esteem, and respect for the system dwindled just a bit more after that unexpected turn of events. I was perplexed. Didn't they want to acquire the best talent for the team, which would ultimately produce a *winning team*? Of course, when my mother caught wind of what had transpired, she sprang into action. Once again, she petitioned the Board of Education. This time, as to why I was not allowed to participate on the varsity baseball team, especially, after I exceeded all tryout expectations. And again, the ruling was in my favor and the coach had to allow me to participate on the baseball varsity squad for that year. The policy was all players had to be given the opportunity to play at least once during the baseball season. Although I was an official player on the varsity team, I still felt it was not a good fit for me socially. I was constantly called racial slurs, and picked on physically, as well as psychologically. I was also banned from the locker room after practice, so I could not take a shower. I had to shower at home. I was frequently restricted from team pep-talks conducted by the coach. I had to sit at a separate area in the dugout and was instructed not to communicate with any of my so-called white colleagues during actual baseball games.

I was benched the whole season, but eventually allowed to play the last strike, of the last out, of the last inning, of the last game.

———— • ————

Age 14 was the age I could apply for working papers, and indeed I did, but with great difficulty and resistance. I was one of the first Black people in my community to apply. I was rejected several times, and finally—with reluctance—I was granted a work permit. I was turned away from all the jobs that did not demand manual labor. I was finally assigned to work the two longest paper routes in the city, with roads that were steep and had the harshest terrain. Although I felt selective discrimination had a huge role in the employment choice assigned to me, it was the only job opportunity available. I performed it with pride. I received my first paycheck and was rather excited to make the mere seventeen dollars for my first two weeks of work. I ventured to a local bank on Main Street, the main commercial strip in New Rochelle, New York. I was met at the door by a white security guard, with his hand firmly on his gun in the holster. He asked me assertively why I was there. I explained to him I had just received my first paycheck from working on my paper route and I wanted to open a bank account. Rudely, he ordered me to stay where I was standing and told me not to move. He went past the bank teller stations before entering a door at the back of the bank. I felt a sense of fear due to the unknown. I wondered why I was being singled out and mistreated. Why were the other patrons at the bank being treated with excellent customer service and respect? Racial discrimination reared its ugly head once again. I was profiled. I was Black and I was the only Black person in the bank. The security guard returned and cautiously escorted me to one of the bank teller's windows. I was forced to sign a document and was told to open a bank account I would have to consent to being fingerprinted. I complied because I did not know any better. Later I discovered that was completely illegal and violated my basic civil rights.

———— • ————

My high school years were quickly approaching. It was a time when the feelings of naiveté should have been fading, and wisdom and maturity should have already taken root. It was an exciting but intimidating transition. There was a larger student population, new teachers, an unfamiliar campus, a more competitive edge, and uncomfortable feelings of displacement. There were more extracurricular activities, additional classes, and lots of clubs to choose from, which caused confusion, indecision, and uncertainty. There were new skills to be mastered and perfecting those skills would help to gain entrance into a great college which in turn would lead to concrete employment opportunities. Some students did a better job adjusting than others. The fear regarding how to overcome and conquer the newfound challenges were real.

I attended New Rochelle High School in New Rochelle, New York. I realized at an early stage, participating in as many academic and extracurricular activities as possible while in high school would lead to a higher level of overall competency. I took advantage of what the school had to offer in programs of academics, sports, clubs, art, theater, and music. I made it my mission to join and participate in as many activities and clubs as time would allow. I joined the gymnastic team. I competed in all-round, but my specialty was rings and vaulting. I placed in the top-three in regionals and state competitions in New York State during the mid-70's. Those skills provided me with the tools to eventually coach Boston University's Men's Gymnastics Team and Fresno State's Women's Gymnastics Team, in which I led them to 3rd in regionals during my college years. In high school, gymnastics was during the winter months. I continued playing baseball which was offered during the spring. Year-round, I was active in the chess club, glee club, Spanish club, French club, fencing club, and Black history club. I was heavily involved in martial arts and received my black belt in Taekwondo. I tried out for every theatre production and landed major character parts in every play. A few of the plays included: Hair, Greece, and Westside Story. I joined the band and became musically proficient in trombone, drums, and guitar. My participation in multiple activities provided an escape from the blatant reality of racism. It was an exhilarating contrast and wonderful change, having contact with students from all ethnic and social backgrounds converging for creative purposes.

Art, music, and sports evokes universal affinity that denotes empathy and compassion, reinforces misunderstood verbal messages, and potentially dispels persistent obstacles that stem from discrimination. This has been a great antidote bringing people from different cultures, social stratospheres, and ethnicities together. It is a remedy which attempts to destigmatize racism. Freedom of expression, the sharing of artistic concepts, melodic ideas, and the fostering of sportsman-like camaraderie helped strike a tremendous blow against racial injustice. In short, this collaboration helped to bring Blacks and whites closer together.

However, my high school years were not devoid of racial incidents. I remember applying for the advanced woodworking class. It was an application/selection process and the person who chose the students for the class, was the woodworking teacher. I was not selected. *Ironically*, I was the only Black applicant. There was a quota as to how many students could attend the class and even after petitioning entrance into the class; I was still rejected.

The last summer after high school was the first summer before college, for some. It was a time of elation and celebration, but for many Black students it was a time of uncertainty and anguish. College acceptance rates and graduation rates have a long history of being low for Black students. Leading up to college, Black youth tend to be less prepared socially, economically, and academically compared to whites. If selected, they tend to be accepted by *substandard* colleges or universities, offering a less than ideal quality of education. They are not equally represented and lack sound credentials in careers such as: law, medicine, engineering, mathematics and physical sciences. They are dissuaded from studying in certain fields, while being encouraged to study in others. This places them at a societal disadvantage *right out of the gate.*

———— • ————

I applied and was accepted to New York State University of Stony Brook. I eventually transferred to Boston University and then transferred to Emerson College in Boston, Massachusetts, where I received a Bachelor of Science in Speech Communications with a Minor in Theatre Arts. I later applied to Fresno State University where I pursued a Masters in Speech Communications. My love for the arts, especially dance and theatre, was compelling. Those memories—other than the times I experienced with my family—have been the most heartfelt and satisfying. I remember them well….

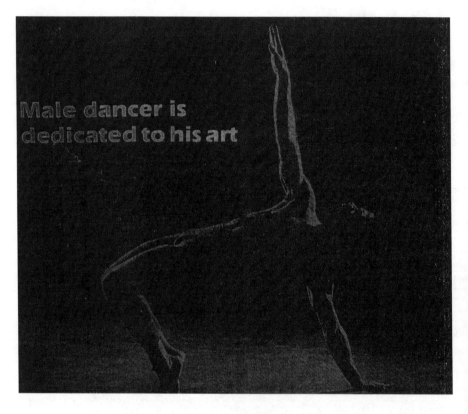

Robert Butler, a member of CSUF's PDT (Portable Dance Troupe)

Robert Butler dance and singing debut in the musical, Greece, at Fresno State University.

A sea of rainbow tights, sweats, and leg warmers adorned the fit women who stood relaxed, yet at attention on the black-painted stage of the John Wright Theater. Their choreographer was busy giving final instructions, trying to get the Portable Dance Troupe (PDT) ready for its March performances at Fresno State University, in 1981.

I was the only man in the group and the only person who was dressed in black tights and a stark white t-shirt, which contrasted against my ebony skin.

I was a dancer. That fact alone put me in a minority. Being the only male dancer in the twelve-member PDT, did not bother me. It did not faze me, and I did not feel any different. My purpose was to dance. My love for dance pulled me closer and closer to the dance department.

During the semester I enrolled in seven dance classes at Fresno State University. I spent an estimated six to eight hours in practice and rehearsal daily. Many of those hours were spent in pain. The pain was immense, but it was a trivial factor. Dancers *like* the pain because it *feels* like progress. A certain amount of suffering is part of getting closer to becoming a great dancer.

Prior to high school I never took one dance class, it just came naturally to me. I took my first dance class during my first year of college in 1976 at Stony Brook University in Long Island, New York. During that time, I performed with the Black Gold Dance Troupe and appeared as Rastus in, "The Day of Absence." My mother became extremely ill during my time at Stony Brook. For several months she had not felt well. She had progressive fatigue, unsettling abdominal pain, and gradual weight loss. After multiple visits to her doctor, she was told her symptoms were due to stress from being overworked. She was advised to rest, take vitamins, and to slow down. She was reassured and convinced by her doctor, stress was the only contributing and causative factor. Blood work was never ordered, imaging studies were never suggested, and her symptoms were continually ignored by her local physician. She continued to get worse. She began having bright red blood in her stool and she had lost over 20 pounds. My mother's skin was ashen, and her eyes took on a yellow hue. She was so weak and frail she needed assistance standing and walking. Her medical condition was emergent. She was transported to Columbia Presbyterian Hospital, a major medical facility in New York City. She was finally evaluated properly, and laboratory tests and imaging studies were ordered. My mother had colon cancer. The shock I felt in that moment was indescribable and the full extent of my mother's illness had not hit home yet. I was angry, sad, bewildered, and numb. Why did her doctor dismiss my mother's progressive symptoms? Why did it take so long for her physician to diagnose a cancer—which if caught early—has a high cure and survival rate?

Why are Black people sicker? Why are Black people misdiagnosed more often and die earlier, than their white counterparts? One of the main factors is the inadequate care

Blacks receive from medical providers. Even when there is adequate insurance and a high level of income and education, there is still a disparity in health care compared to whites. Because of the lack of appropriate healthcare access, Blacks are more likely to die from cancer, cardiovascular disease, and diabetes. Black women are less likely to receive chemotherapy and radiation for cancer treatment, compared to white women. This is partly due to provider bias. White physicians have internal biases—conscious or unconscious—which projects in providing inferior health care to minority populations. There are also structural, socioeconomic factors which contribute to discriminatory disparities in Black healthcare. Neighborhoods are often segregated with white physicians gravitating toward practicing in white neighborhoods. There is basically a two-tiered healthcare system, which provides quality healthcare to those with private healthcare insurance, and suboptimal healthcare to those on a subsidized insurance plan like: Medi-Cal.

My mother finally received the long overdue medical care she needed. She had a surgical procedure called a partial colectomy. She did not receive chemotherapy or radiation treatments and was sent home to recuperate. I had to quit college and return to New Rochelle, New York to care for her. I did not want to give up my education or dance, so I worked odd jobs and enrolled in educational classes at Westchester Community College when I could. I kept up my dancing by taking classes in ballet, modern dance, and jazz.

I had the distinct opportunity to briefly train with Mikhail Baryshnikov who is the leading ballet dancer in the world; and Martha Graham who was an influential American dancer, teacher, and modern dance choreographer. The training was grueling, but it enabled me to perfect my technical dance skills. In combination, my dance expression improved, and it helped me to exude heightened emotion through performance.

I felt like dancing was an innate, natural force within me which compelled me to take this avenue. It was a hard road, a difficult path. It was in my blood. It kept me connected to the realities of life.

When the New York Dance Festival rolled around, I was scheduled to perform. But two days before the show, I broke both my ankles riding down a hill on a skateboard. Somehow the screws came loose on the skateboard and I slammed onto the ground. I had to crawl several hundred yards to get home.

The injury prevented me from dancing for seven months. To this day, my right ankle is still not as flexible as it was prior to the accident.

My mother regained her health. She was in remission. In 1977 I moved away from home and transferred to Boston University where I was accepted into their theatrical program. I was one of only a few Black students to qualify for admission to the program. At that time, I appeared as "The Dancer" in "Never, Never Land." I also danced for a short time with The

Boston Ballet.

Times were difficult. The winter of '77 to '78 brought the terrible blizzard. I will never forget it. Snow was packed 12 feet high. Trucks could not come into the city and cars could not get out. It was the time when the Russian Flu pandemic devastated the world. I caught it. The electricity went out city-wide for days. It created an environment of pure fear and anxiety. The local grocery stores began to ration food. The rations per person, per day included: six eggs, a quart of milk, and a loaf of bread. All the shelves in the stores were constantly bare. There were no canned foods or goodies to be found. Just when I thought things could not get worse, I was kicked out of my apartment because my two roommates did not keep up with their portion of the rent. I remember developing a 103-degree fever with extreme chills and overwhelming fatigue. I had nowhere to go for shelter or food. The only place I could think of was the Boston Student Union Hall. They allowed me to rest and reside in their back office for several days, until winter break. I was able to eat and sleep there in exchange for bussing tables and cleaning dishes during and after cafeteria hours.

When I returned home at the beginning of winter break, I was extremely weak with severe malnutrition and dehydration. I spent two weeks in the hospital and two weeks bedridden at home.

Through all of this, I was still highly motivated to return to school and resume my passion for the arts. Although my love for the arts was still strong, I began to focus on a major in Speech Communications. I transferred to Emerson College in 1978. This was an excellent communications college and had a formidable arts program as well. Impetus to transfer stemmed from the memory of my childhood speech issues. It was during this time, I tried out for the national touring company: "A Chorus Line."

Over 200 men tried out for various roles. I remember being divided into groups of 50 to audition. The group of 200 was cut to 60, and I qualified. The next cut lowered the number to 20. We then had to audition in groups of 4. I was in the first group. I was asked to step forward, state my name, my hobbies, and my experience. I recited my small list of credits to the director. Standing next to me was the dancer next in line to audition. He stepped forward and shared about his performances in: "Bubbling Brown Sugar" and "Evita." They took the people with experience.

I was not discouraged. I continued my training and career in the arts. My *curriculum vitae* continued to grow.

My performances with the PDT, while at Fresno State prior, were some of my most challenging. "Dream was one of the performances and it was composed to music by the percussion group. It was challenging because of the different elements. It was the most visually exciting due to the element of scenic design. In the choreography, each dancer was given an animal to enact. I enacted a reptile. It was as if we became our given animals through dance. Our *spirit animals*.

I had a passion to express myself to people through dance. I thought about it all the time. My mind was always *moving* and so was my body. A dancer's work is never done. Dance, for me, fulfilled the cravings I had for communicating with people of all types.

This was a time when it seemed racial indifference was not recognized, or merely just an illusion. Nonetheless, working together, side by side, was commonplace in the arts for both Blacks and whites. Creative progress was not hindered because there seemed to be no issues with color and diversity.

CHAPTER 3

"Music calms the average beast," but violence kills the average Black. Police violence against blacks is institutionally and fundamentally problematic. It is wrong! It is disproportionate in Blacks compared to whites, with an unprecedented number of Black people killed yearly compared to white people. There are no judicial safeguards or processes built into the system which fairly addresses this disparity. Racist Black codes, slave patrols, and Jim Crow Laws of the past were inherently built into police institutions. White vigilantes and lynching mobs killed thousands of innocent Blacks throughout history. The judicial system was an all-white enterprise, thus white vigilantes often went unpunished. The civil rights era and the Black Life Matters movement of today, attempted to incorporate into its arsenal of defense, peaceful demonstration, but this was and is, often squashed by police brutality.

Many blacks still succumb to the overt violence and silent racism of police brutality: Mike Brown who was shot with his hands up surrendering; Eric Garner who was placed in a choke hold and died; Tamir Rice, a 12 year old, who was shot while holding a toy gun; Alton Sterling and Philando Castile who were shot within days of each other; George Floyd who died by a knee on his neck while begging to breathe. These are a few of the multitude of Blacks who were senselessly killed at the hands of police.

Not all cops are bad, but there is a silent code of camaraderie which prevents them from outrightly intervening during episodes of misconduct by their fellow officers.

———— • ————

I have always been a baseball fan and 1977 was an amazing year for baseball. I was in college at Boston University, the year the New York Yankees beat the Red Sox for the pennant. Being a New Yorker, I was elated. I remember the excitement my two roommates—who also happened to be black—and I expressed when the Yankees won. We were at a sports bar. Suddenly, we heard, "Kill the Niggers." There was a group of white people who were upset that their team did not secure the win. We were chased out of the bar. We were pursued for at least 15 to 20 blocks past several police officers who blatantly ignored our peril. We ran for our lives and finally lost them. Nobody helped us. Nobody cared.

I had the opportunity to move into a large 3-bedroom house with my two roommates, in Dorchester, Massachusetts while attending Boston University. It was about 35 minutes from campus on the orange line trolley system, followed by a one mile walk to the house from the trolley station. It was a far cry from living in a one bedroom in the heart of Boston, shared by three students. We finally moved in but quickly came to realize we were the only Black residents in an all-white neighborhood. We were not universally accepted. We were not wanted. We were fearful and extremely uncomfortable every time we came home by trolley at the end of a long day of classes. Every day we were called derogatory names. "Niggers get out, " was shouted at us repeatedly. Most nights we experienced rocks and bottles being hurled at us while we ran home to escape the onslaught. We reported this to the local police precinct, and instead of helping us, they recommended we move out of the neighborhood. We only lasted one month in that house.

In 1981, while attending Fresno State University, I often visited Santa Clara just to get away. I remember traveling with my two friends. We were driving through an affluent neighborhood in Santa Clara, when suddenly, several police cars converged on us with their sirens blaring. We quickly pulled over. We were frantic, and before we realized what was transpiring; we were forcefully dragged from the car, handcuffed, and pushed face down onto the asphalt, with a cop's foot pressed against the side of each of our heads. Three black males had just robbed a bank in Santa Clara. We fit the descriptions. It was a horrifying encounter that seemed to last an eternity. The Police Sergeant looked down and gazed at one of my friends who glanced up at the same time. They recognized each other. They were friends! We were lifted off the hot asphalt and a few insincere apologies were muttered as the police walked away.

———— • ————

During my time at Fresno State I was involved with the Upward Bound program. It was funded by the US Department of Education. The program provided high school students, from low income families, with a pre-college curriculum that supported and helped them succeed in their educational pursuits. The goal of the program was to increase the rate of high school students completing a secondary level of education, and to ultimately enroll them in, and have them graduate from, postsecondary education programs. The program also offered: after school tutorials, academic advising, college conferences, university campus tours, parent meetings, college admission application assistance, ACT/SAT fee waivers, career planning, financial aid application assistance, community service, a summer residential program at Fresno State, academic courses, summer internships/jobs, stipend checks, career guest speakers, and cultural exposure.

I applied for my Class 2 driver's license. I woke up every Saturday morning at 4 a.m. and drove a van to pick up Black and migrant worker students for Upward Bound. The students were from Fresno, Clovis, Sanger, and Madera. I was integrally responsible for structuring, formulating, organizing, and teaching an academic curriculum. It was a true educational experience and a great opportunity for the participants and for *me*!

The positive aspects of education are far reaching. It plants the seed for educational growth which ultimately will provide the tools for future success. It fosters a sense of accomplishment, builds character, promotes self-esteem, boosts self- confidence, and reinforces positive attitudes.

This was an extremely enjoyable time for me. I wanted to share the gift of education and the program granted me this. I was amazed how much intellect and talent those young kids possessed *and* how quickly they became proficient in what they were learning.

The positive learning environment was marred by a terrible incident that occurred in Clovis one dark night. A fourteen-year-old migrant worker's son was found hanging from a tree. He had a noose around his neck. The devastation was far reaching. Fear and speculation ran rampant. There was a sense of uneasiness and anger because the same day the horrible hanging took place, the Invincible Empire, and the United Klans of America sponsored a march in Clovis. Two more marches took place; one in Merced, California and one in Fresno, California, just a few days later. Peaceful demonstrations against the meaning of what the KKK stood for eventually turned violent. Fights broke out between the two opposing sides. The police, who stand for justice and fairness *for all,* provided protection for the Klan members. Many of the demonstrators, who were of minority status, were arrested for disturbing the peace and inciting a riot.

The KKK has had a long history of violence. Black people were the main focus of their hate. However, Jews, Catholics, immigrants, and the LGBTQ population also became victims of their hate crimes. The Klan was responsible for numerous atrocities; lynching's, rapes, and tarring-and-feathering were commonplace. Their infiltration into the judicial system allowed them to commit these acts of violence without punishment. The Klan was responsible for the 16th Street Baptist Church incident, where four young Black girls were killed while attending Sunday services.

———— • ————

I remember, one cold winter morning, taking the bus to Copley Square in Boston, Massachusetts. I was going to an interview for an internship position. I arrived at the office building, walked into the warm lobby, and brushed the wet snow off my winter coat. I proceeded to the elevators. The elevator doors opened, and I stepped in. To the left of me was a mother and her five-year-old son. The little boy inquisitively looked up at his mother. He said, "Mommy, why is his skin black?" His mother's face turned red with embarrassment, as she trembled with fear, while she attempted to cover her son's mouth with her hand. She had clearly anticipated an aggressive, retaliatory response. However, I looked at them both empathetically and said, "He is just a child and I take no offense." The air had been cleared. There is an obvious gap in perception between whites and Blacks. Whites view Blacks as stereotypically different...as victimizers, but never victims. Black people are often prejudged as being hostile, angry, and verbally confrontational. Although some whites realize prejudice and racial discrimination are problems, it is a minority consensus. They feel the Black community brings these problems on themselves. White sentiment seems to portray Blacks as always having a chip on their shoulders. Stereotyping is common due to the way Black people physically appear, from their facial features to their hair texture. Blacks are also deemed as lazy, less intelligent, and having no work ethic. White consensus points toward their annoyance that Black people receive special breaks in financial assistance, education, and employment. There is a vicious cycle of negativity between whites and Blacks, but no true actions to fix the ongoing, broken-down race relations. The hostility and resentment between the two races are at a standstill and until white people understand what it is like to be Black in America, the divide will never end.

———— • ————

During the summer months in-between college, I worked in New Rochelle at the Parks and Recreation Department. I worked with my younger sister and two close friends. We were responsible for developing community programs and activities to bridge the gaps between the young and the old in the community. The summers I worked developing and implementing the program, were incredibly rewarding. It was an opportunity to give back to my community. Although the pay was not much, I gained wealth in satisfaction. We were issued retired government vehicles which did not have any city registration. The vehicles were used for transportation around town. I remember the four of us driving to a community project we were working on. Suddenly, the sound of sirens echoed behind us. There was a police car following us. I was the one driving and I quickly pulled over. I promptly and cautiously placed both of my hands on the steering wheel. A white police officer approached the car. He glared at me as I slowly rolled down the window. He asked for the registration of the car. I politely replied by reminding him, city vehicles did not have registrations. The police officer became highly agitated and extremely angry. He abruptly opened the car door, pulled me out, and slammed me headfirst into the ground. During this incident, he repeatedly kicked me in my groin. While I was on the ground, he stated I was under arrest, as he continued to tighten the cuffs around my wrists to the point where I lost all sensation in my hands. He did not read me my Miranda Rights. I was terrified and scared. I thought I was going to die. I thought I was going to be another sad statistic. I did not resist or provide any verbal response. I did not want to give him any motive for additional physical abuse. I laid limp, like a rag doll, and just *absorbed* every, painful kick. I was transported to the local police station and dragged in by my handcuffs. While I pleaded for the officer to stop, I repeatedly made mention that I was home for the summer from college and I worked for Parks and Recreation. I was checked for any priors. Of course, I was clean. Fortunately, the Director of Parks and Recreation was a close friend of the family. He was summoned to the police station. He verified my story and I was reluctantly released without a hint of apology.

It did not end there. There was a constant barrage of police harassment after being released from the station for false imprisonment. Police harassment is commonplace; arbitrarily stopping someone, aggressively questioning him or her, or conducting unwarranted illegal search and seizure seemed like a daily practice. Day and night unmarked police vehicles parked one to two blocks from our home. We were under constant surveillance. I was pulled over countless times by police officers for trivial and absurd reasons. They summoned me out of the vehicle and demanded I place my hands on the side of the car. They aggressively kicked my legs open to assume *the stance*. I was instructed not to move and if I did, I was hit by one of their police batons on my back and legs. The pain was unbearable. They unlawfully searched the vehicle from front to back. I was detained approximately 30-40 minutes each time. We also received death threats at all hours of the day and night by phone. Sometimes the phone rang relentlessly for hours on end. When answered, derogatory slurs came from the other end of the line; "You are all dead Niggers and you're going to wish you were never born Niggers." Sometimes there were several minutes of silence at a time. The statements were unforgettable and expressed the unfounded hate and resentment they had for people of color. There was no one or nowhere to turn to, to report the endless harassment. The police department, which was the institution that had vowed to serve and protect, was the very institution that harassed and terrorized us. Disciplinary procedures against police officers have long been a source of frustration. The system has fallen short of holding officers accountable for their misdeeds, actions, and behaviors. They get away with it because they *can.*

Racial prejudice stems from the fear of misunderstanding people of different social groups. This can be out-right, on a subconscious level, or maybe a biological predisposition. There are no quick and easy solutions to this puzzling problem, but by reducing the fear of racism we can hopefully dispel fallacious myths and decrease or eliminate the violence that racism often creates. Racism is a systemic reality. It lives and breathes discrimination and oppression throughout all communities. It victimizes people of color and encourages the privilege of white people. The system of oppression can produce low self-confidence, self-hatred, and low self-esteem. The subtleties of racism, profiling, and stereotyping creates a demoralizing sense of nonacceptance.

———— • ————

Tragically, my mother's cancer returned. I was living in Fresno, in 1982, when I received the news. She had advanced colon cancer which metastasized to her liver and throughout her whole body. I worked as many odd jobs as possible to raise the money to travel to New York to be with her. I made five hundred dollars, which was enough to purchase a used car. It was a 1976 Honda 1488 CC Civic Hatchback. I packed the necessities and ventured off to New York. I drove nonstop across Route 80 without sleep and with minimal food. When I reached the state of Iowa, I heard a loud sound underneath my car. There was smoke everywhere and my car came to a sudden halt. The engine rod had blown. I had to leave the car on the side of the road with all my belongings, and I hitchhiked the rest of the way home.

The pain and anguish I felt thinking about my mother's condition while driving across country was immense. It was a surreal feeling knowing that my mother had a terminal illness which did not discriminate or care about skin color. The overwhelming reality finally set in when I arrived in New York. It took me three days and twenty hours to arrive. My mother was frail and weak but was energized with enthusiasm when I walked through the front door. I fought back tears as I hugged her. This was a difficult new chapter in my life. I helped support my parents any way I could. My father owned a 1976 Datsun B210. It was the only transportation we had. I would wake up every morning at 4 a.m. to drop my father off at work. He worked at Columbia-Presbyterian Hospital in New York City. He was the chief engineer for a company called Electronics for Medicine. He was responsible for maintaining the functionality of all the major hospital equipment. After dropping him off, I ventured back home to care for my mother and take her to her chemotherapy sessions. I would then drive back to pick up my father from work by 5:30 p.m. I did this for several months, until one day, the engine of the only car we had, seized up. This happened during winter. I sold all my belongings and raised enough money to purchase a used engine from a local junkyard. I rented a hoist and bought all the parts needed to help rebuild the engine. There was no door on our garage, so I put plastic over the opening to keep the cold out while I worked on the car. I prepped the car, hoisted the engine up, and lowered it into the Datsun B210. I turned the key with anticipation, the car started, and I was able to continue fulfilling my parent's transportation needs.

Seeing my mother suffer through her illness was a hard thing to swallow. She moaned constantly because of her uncontrollable pain. She had to rely on help 24 hours a day. The frequent nausea, vomiting, abdominal pain, and diarrhea gave her little rest. The chemotherapy caused extreme exhaustion and her hair to fall out. This was one of the lowest points in my life. My mother was suffering, *and* I did not know if I would be able to complete my education. One of the days I drove my father to work, he asked me to come in to meet someone. The person was one of my father's coworkers. He was a MD/PhD who was Head of the Anesthesiology Department and a researcher at Columbia-Presbyterian Hospital in New York City. I was offered an assistant research position. This sparked an interest in medicine for me.

———— • ————

I visited Iona College in New Rochelle, New York. It was a four-year accredited college. My goal was to take the prerequisite courses for entrance into medical school in one year, even though it was a two-year curriculum. I was met by one of the clergy student advisors. I expressed my goal. He responded with a look of astonishment on his face. He referred to *my kind* as having the intellectual incapacity to complete such a feat. This was a prime example of racial stereotyping based on skin color alone. My goal, after that incident, was to prove him wrong by achieving everything I shared with him and then some.

I also visited Westchester Community College in Valhalla, New York which was sponsored by Westchester County and the State University of New York. It had a full-service academic institution which provided students with extra academic support. They also had transfer agreements with multiple institutions and private colleges. The school had a multidisciplinary curriculum, most importantly, it offered exactly what I was looking for, a strong emphasis on the medical sciences.

I remember walking into the Dean's office. A tall, distinguished man of African American descent greeted me. His name was Dean Ford. His was a name I will never forget. I expressed my one-year goal of taking all prerequisites for premed and applying to medical school. Dean Ford was excited. He had never had a student request a different route of study to achieve such a goal. He devised a special curriculum for me and created a medical school board of professors, from each of the premed disciplines, to help guide me through my studies. He also created a medical school file for me and with the assistance of his secretary, helped me fill out the applications and mail them off to various medical schools throughout the country. He even covered all the application expenses. He then provided me with a full scholarship and a job as a Teacher's Assistant.

———— • ————

My mother qualified for transportation services for her chemotherapy sessions. My father used the car for work. I walked two miles to the bus stop every morning to attend school. I started with summer school. I took Organic Chemistry and Inorganic Chemistry at the same time. It was a 6-week session. I carried a double course load during the academic school year by taking: Anatomy & Physiology, Cell Biology, Physics, Microbiology, and Biochemistry. I maintained a 3.96 GPA. I worked as a teacher's assistant in the Biology lab during the day and I worked for MCI, as a communications specialist from 6:00-10:00 p.m. at night. I took the bus back and walked the two miles home. At times, when I did not have enough money to take the bus, I hitchhiked the twenty miles it took to get to school. I was motivated. I was determined.

Achievements that Black students made in education were often overlooked. Despite many obstacles, Black students have excelled in education.

I completed my premed course work in one year. I had made my one-year goal and I did it despite overwhelming obstacles. The Dean's office processed ten medical school applications for me. I applied to nine schools in California and one in New York. I received interview replies from UCLA and the University of California, Irvine.

It was a time of reckoning. It was a time when I felt cultural differences were set aside and my achievements were due to personal merit and unwavering perseverance. Socioeconomic and educational inequities were temporarily overcome.

The interview process was arduous because I did not have enough money to travel to California. I applied for a credit card and was accepted. I charged a plane ticket, hotel accommodations, a rental car, and meals. When all was said and done, I ended up charging close to three thousand dollars on my credit card. It took me approximately seven years to pay it off.

My first interview at UCLA was an unforgettable experience. I drove up to the campus, pulled into the parking lot, and anticipated a successful interview experience. My senses were heightened while I walked up the stairs to the interviewer's office. I walked into the room and noticed a large, mahogany desk, and behind it, a tall leather office chair with its back facing me. The chair never turned around. I heard the words, "Apply again next year." That was it? That was the end of the interview? I turned around and walked out of the room. I felt a huge sense of defeat. All the hard work, all the effort, and all the expense. I had to keep a positive outlook. I still had another opportunity. I had the interview with Irvine coming up in two days. I prepared myself for the next interview. I walked into the student center where the interviews were conducted. I introduced myself and I was told to wait in the student area for a moment. I was filled with nervous excitement. I was almost there. Five minutes of waiting seemed like hours. A staff member returned and informed me they were not taking any more interviews. The rejection was overwhelming. My demeanor went from standing up straight with excitement, to slumped with disappointment. I was devastated. How could this happen? Why did this happen? I guess I will never know. I thought I was a strong medical school candidate. Although I was granted two interviews, I did not make it through one. Deep down I knew why.

It was a long airplane ride back to New York full of speculation and bewilderment. My first inclination was to give up the notion of ever becoming a doctor. I toiled and contemplated which direction to go regarding a career path. I arrived home. I walked through the door to see one lone letter sitting on the kitchen table. It was from New York Medical College. My hands were shaking, and my heart was pounding. It was my last chance. It was an acceptance letter for entrance into their medical school! The acceptance was based on application review alone and no interview was required. I quivered with excitement. No, I screamed with excitement at the top of my lungs! I was accepted into medical school, wow! Again, all the hard work, pushing myself to the limit when I was too exhausted to do so…I was going to medical school!

———— • ————

The first day of medical school was spent in orientation. I entered in 1986 with 207 other students. The class of 1990 graduated 194 doctors. There was a collective sea of students from different demographics, backgrounds, and cultures. However, there were only seventeen minorities and three were African American. The rest of the minority make-up were from the Islands, more specifically: Jamaica, Grenada, West Indies, Barbados, and the Bahamas. The Associate Dean of Minority Affairs was West Indian and he ran a tight ship academically. My major in college was not concentrated in the sciences, but in communications and the arts. I recall a comment made to me by the Dean, "These medical students will eat you up and spit you out." Maybe this was an initial attempt to spark fear into me, or maybe it was to wake up my cognitive skills to keep me on guard through the tough four years? Whatever the reasoning, I was overjoyed to attend medical school.

Robert's New York Medical College ID badge.

I struggled financially in medical school. I did not have financial assistance from my parents and financial aid was limited. I visited the financial aid office for assistance but there was no aid left. I was told ten minority scholarships were available.

They were granted to minority medical students each year and were given out by the Associate Dean of Minority Affairs. I was somewhat concerned about how I would be able to afford medical school for four years with the high tuition, room, board, and other miscellaneous expenses. In my freshman year, I was bold enough to ask the Associate Dean of Minority Affairs for one of the minority scholarships. He was responsible for choosing which students qualified for and received the scholarships. I was turned down.

Medical students often gathered at the student recreation center on campus. It was a place where students could relax, play games, or just study. Ping-pong was one of the most popular games played. It sharpened the reflexes and heightened the competitive edge. It was a great way of letting go of stress and frustration. The Associate Dean of Minority Affairs was the undisputed champion in ping-pong. No one had ever beaten him. He had defeated every student who challenged him. Still desperate for financial assistance, I challenged him to a ping-pong match. The contingency was; if I won, he was to grant me a minority scholarship. His ego took over and he accepted my challenge. The game commenced with all the medical students watching the match to see who would win. A lot was at stake. The first opponent to reach twenty-one by two points, would be the winner. I was down nineteen to eleven. Amazingly, I raked up nine points in a row. The score was twenty to nineteen in my favor. I reached twenty-one to his nineteen and won the match! I did it! I won! Loud cheers erupted as the medical students congratulated me. My opponent humbly thanked me for a great game. I gained a newfound respect from him. Per our agreement, I received the tenth and last minority scholarship for the year. I received $10,000 my freshman year and $10,000 each subsequent three years. The scholarship helped my financial situation immensely. I supplemented the rest of my expenses with loans and grants.

I graduated from New York Medical College in 1990 and *matched* in Family Practice at the University of Minnesota's Residency Program.

Two incidents occurred during Medical School, both of which left an indelible blemish in my memory. It was the start of the third year at New York Medical College. Those were the clinical years. The first two years of basic sciences were complete. I was a young clinician. I was eager to put into action what I learned during my medical school basic science curriculum. I was ready to start but hard work was ahead. I woke up each morning at 3 a.m., I grabbed a pushcart and collected the eighteen or more patient charts to complete the pre-round *scut work* prior to formal rounds with the Attending. The formal rounds started at 8 a.m. I had to examine patients, write notes, and complete orders. I had to draw my own patient blood samples, print labels for the tubes, and personally bring them to the laboratory. Once the laboratory tests were analyzed, I had to pick up the spreadsheets and interpret them. I had to wheel the patients on gurneys, to the radiology department for their x-rays, and then wheel them back to their rooms when they were done. Once the x-rays were completed and read by the radiologist, I had to return to the radiology department to pick up all the x-ray jackets. I had to prepare and present each patient to the Attending Physician with subjective and objective findings concerning the patient's clinical condition, along with lab and radiographic interpretation. I also had to formulate an assessment and plan of care and provide treatment options. This was a four hour process each morning during the clinical rotations.

My first patient I rounded on, in a group of eight third year medical students, was an 87-year-old white male. I remember his frail body and his weakened state of health. The patient: in a soft, raspy, low, voice muttered, "I don't want that Nigger touching me." Gasps of surprise came from my fellow students. Sadly, what he said was not unusual to me. I showed respect and walked out of the exam room. Just like that, the patient was assigned to another medical student.

The surgery rotation was one of my favorite rotations. It provided great hands-on experience. It enhanced technical skills, dexterity, and problem-solving skills. We had an intriguing vascular surgical case. I was asked by the Surgical Attending to assist. I began to prep by sterile technique. Medical staff assisted me in putting on sterile scrubs and gloves. I entered the surgery suite and was met by a surgical registered nurse. She said, "Thanks for coming to clean the room, the garbage is over there." She thought I was the janitor, but I was a third-year medical student who just happened to be Black. The Attending reprimanded the nurse and demanded I receive an apology from her for the misrepresentation.

Fortunately, I have beaten many odds and overcome a multitude of challenges that could have hindered my acceptance to, and progression through, medical school. But other Black students were not as fortunate. There is a huge disparity and a much smaller percentage of Black students entering medical schools compared to whites. Systemic racism begets socioeconomic deterrents, which decreases educational opportunities and perpetuates the belief that Black students lack the intellectual skills to compete on the same level as white students in medicine.

Medical schools have attempted to allocate scoring systems and provide special scholarships to help enroll more Black students. Graduating more Black medical doctors can ultimately level out the health disparities in Black communities.

Medical school provided me with a myriad of experiences. Some I will never forget. There were highs and there were lows, but my determination to succeed was unwavering. It was also the time when I received the worst news of my life. I was in the Anatomy lab. It was my first year of medical school, October of 1986. I was studying for the Anatomy midterm practicum. A faculty member walked in and gave me the news. My mother had passed away. I was devastated. My eyes teared up, my heart pulsated, and I began to tremble uncontrollably. I dropped to my knees in hysterics. Mother had succumbed to cancer. My disbelief was overwhelming, and the reality was surreal. I remember my classmates picking me up off the floor to console me. The hugs were plentiful. My mother died in Tallahassee, Florida, where she was born. I did not have enough money to purchase an airplane ticket to attend the funeral. Surprisingly, my classmates raised $107 for a round-trip ticket. I will never forget their generosity and concern.

CHAPTER 4

Racial polarization between whites and Blacks during the 1990's and 2000's, were increasingly evident. There was no doubt racism existed and maintained the divide. Racism was a destructive force that permeated society. Black people have not been considered an integral part of society and have been stereotyped as socially indifferent and politically inept. Policies which portended to help minorities, were often ignored by the very people who promoted equal justice for all. The notion that blacks and whites were equal under the law seemingly stemmed from *fantasy*, like a lengthy piece of fiction with no end. The construct of racism was more widespread than just within the sociopolitical arena. It was far reaching, in all aspects of life.

———— • ————

Racism in America is still alive and well. It prevents equality and fairness for the few who are not accepted and do not fit in due to societal perceptions. It is inherently wrong and unfortunately built into the DNA of America. As long as we continue to turn a blind eye to the pain of those suffering under its oppression, we will never escape its origins. *Justice* has a different definition for people of color. Discrimination against the Black community still affects employment and housing opportunities. It continues to contribute to the increase in Black incarceration and prosecution rates.

The socioeconomic disparities racism creates can be seen in every spectrum of society. During the last two to three decades, however, there has been some change. Black people have made advancements in obtaining more suitable employment opportunities and higher paying jobs; but still make up the highest percentage of the poor. Black people have held more political positions; but still make up the highest prison incarceration rates in comparison to whites. College graduation rates have steadily been on the rise among Black students; but they still have the lowest high school graduation rates. America's continued inequity and its discriminatory undertones continues to interfere with important policies that could advance the Black community, such as: affirmative action and educational reform.

There is speculation white racism is the causative root for many problems which concern race relations in the nation today, but some also speculate the racial divide is narrowing between whites and Blacks. It is important to note, however, no matter how much optimism is *in the air*; it is false optimism. Black people still feel the extent of racism, with its persistent racial stereotyping, unrelenting discrimination, silent segregation, and never-ending alienation. Indeed, racism still exists and the false notion that America is color-blind is a misnomer. Racism and its societal rejection of Black people may often be subliminal, and prejudice may not always be a conscious realization by those who practice it. However, whatever theories formulate in, and attempt to explain the evil of racism; skin color plays the biggest roll in its propagation. Racism is a breeding ground for prejudice and prejudice produces an ideology that being different is not acceptable and being the same is. This creates a dichotomy of social class. The outcome is the development of groups of people categorized as either superior or inferior. This *diversity*, and the racial hate it produces, is fueled by intolerance, selfish intentions, self-interest, mistrust, fear, and ignorance. The goal is to bring these two opposing groups together and create peaceful dialogue in hopes of bridging the racial divide which has long been a destructive force in America.

———— • ————

As I dealt with the times and the ongoing issues of racism, my focus was medical school. This was a time when simulated medical study and laboratory course work, as a medical student, would be met with practical hands-on clinical experience. Initially, it was difficult to understand what my role would be, but after my first few days of residency I realized I was no longer a medical student but a bona fide medical resident. I was a physician under the supervision of a physician and the only way I was going to learn medicine was through experience and mentorship. I knew it was going to be three of the most grueling years of my life, but I was up for the task. I realized each minute, hour, day, week, month, and year spent learning in residency brought me closer and closer to graduating as a practicing medical doctor. I was certain residency would be tough and chaotic, but I recognized my strong post graduate training would be integral in getting me through the program. Years of cumulative hard work would lead to a lifelong journey of caring for people. Learning how to communicate, coordinate care, write clinical notes, consult with fellow physicians, arrange family meetings, attend clinical meetings, and grand rounds was all part of the integrative learning process. There were times when the frustration and stress was overwhelming, but this too was part of the process. A resident had to find ways to balance life and work. Mental, physical, and emotional wellness was important to maintain, in order to prevent psychological and physical breakdown.

There were times, however, when I was not treated as equal compared to the white residents. I was often belittled by Attending Physicians during daily rounds, and in front of other residents when presenting at grand rounds. I was ostracized and not allowed to participate in certain clinical research projects, and I was given the scut jobs that no one wanted to sign up for. I was never given my first choice of vacation and always placed on the rounding schedule for all the major holidays. I was often identified as a janitor and many times called over by staff members to assist in cleaning up soiled rooms and to take out trash. I had patients refuse to be touched by me and demanded to be cared for by a white doctor. Derogatory comments and slurs were often hurled at me, by patients, out loud and under their breath. I was not fully accepted and could not act freely as a true resident compared to the white residents. There was truly a disparity in fairness. The discrimination I encountered was obviously due to the color of my skin. It was hurtful and demeaning.

———— • ————

Setting up living arrangements was difficult to achieve prior to starting my residency in Minneapolis, Minnesota. I filled out multiple rental applications and was denied housing by almost everyone. I was given many excuses as to why I was denied. I was told a mistake was made and the apartment was already rented. I was blatantly told, "We don't rent to your kind." There were instances when I was shown an apartment with a beautiful view overlooking great landscapes, but when I came back to sign the lease, it was for a smaller apartment in the rear of the apartment complex with little or no view. Many times, I never heard back from the rental office at all. Racial discrimination and disparity in fair housing has long been a problematic issue. Its controversy needs little introduction. It has been and still is, woven into the fabric of all communities in America. Prior to the Fair Housing Act of 1968 there was the systemic use of property deeds to enforce racial segregation. This was done through mapping. The maps helped people visualize the settlement and the spread of minorities demographically. They were called racial covenants which had contractual verbiage that restricted the sale of certain homes or properties to people of color. Minnesota's Mapping Project has been integral in providing a foundation for understanding the importance of reversing and further preventing racist housing trends in communities.

I graduated in 1990 from the University of Minnesota, in Family Practice. This was an exciting time for me. I knew all the hard work sacrifice and studying finally paid off. I had the daunting task of deciding which direction to take after residency. There were a multitude of career paths to choose from. Doing clinical research was an option. Extending out my studies by applying for a one, or two-year fellowship and sub-specializing in a discipline of medicine was another viable option. Some residents, after graduating, put great effort into starting a private practice. Most residents, however, opted to start their practice in a clinic or hospital setting.

During my over 30 years in practice, I have worked in urgent cares, community clinics, as a hospitalist, and in an emergency room setting. The work experiences have been equally rewarding. However, being a Black doctor was not always easy. Black doctors frequently experience patients requesting to be cared for by a doctor of a particular race. It could be subtle or outright blatant.

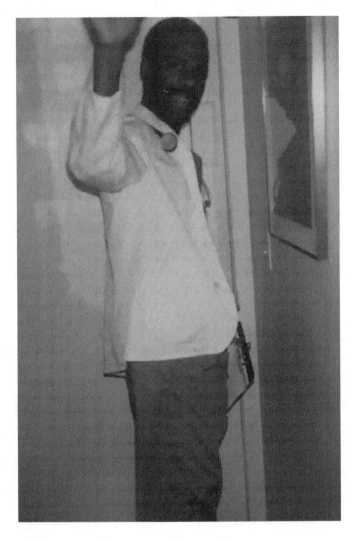

Robert Butler in his first year of residency at University of Minnesota.

Although it is the patient's right to choose a doctor of a particular skin color, it is still discrimination. Some argue that a request for a white physician is in accordance with the ethical principle of patient autonomy. Nonetheless, it is morally and ethically unjustified. The nation's long history of racism has been a painful thread in the history of medicine. It has created an environment of distrust, it has lowered the number of Black students wanting to become physicians, and it has widened the disparity of access to good clinical care in Black communities. Conversely, there were times when my colleagues had difficulty accepting me simply because I am Black. I was often excluded from certain group activities and I was not invited to events after work. When choosing a hospital rounding team, I felt an air of reluctance by my team members after I had been placed on their team. My clinical skills and intellect had often been undermined and disrespectfully criticized by doctors and nurses alike, even though there were no clinical flaws. I received emails referring to me as, "substandard," from a colleague I worked with who was considered my equal. I repeatedly heard from a certain medical director, "Blacks need extra clinical guidance," yet never heard this repeated to the white doctors who worked right alongside me. This was a double standard that was motivated by and expressed through *silent racism*. There were times when I was asked if I needed extra time or assistance to complete a task, even though I was overly accomplished at it already. I have had nurses—who don't have the same level of clinical training—barge into my office and scold me regarding why I had chosen a particular clinical path for a patient, without knowing the facts of the case. This suggests Black doctors are less capable than white doctors and just *not good enough*. While rounding in the hospital, preparing to write a note on a patient I was assigned to, the Attending Specialist questioned who I was and why I was attending to his patient. He referred to *my kind* as not being capable of caring for a complicated patient. He assigned the patient to a white internist who was sitting next to me. Title VII of the Civil Rights Act of 1964 prohibits employers from assigning work based on employee race.

There was another incident I will never forget. A new Medical Director had just been assigned to the clinic. He seemed of good character and interacted well with the staff. Weeks passed and it seemed like he would be a good fit for the clinic. Then, a strange, unfathomable incident occurred. I was in my office and I stood up from my desk to prepare myself for my next patient. I felt a breath on the back of my neck and heard a whisper, "Why do you Niggers exist." I was surprised, shocked, and stunned! I turned around quickly and saw the Medical Director staring at me. With a blank expression on his face, he turned on his heels and walked away like nothing had happened. I could not wrap my brain around what I had experienced in that moment.

Then, there was a charity sponsored golf tournament at Riverwalk Golf Course in San Diego, California. I was practicing on the putting green prior to tee off time. Suddenly, I heard whispering in my ear, "How do you and Tiger Woods exist in this world." It was the same Medical Director who had made the previous derogatory comments! I could not believe it. What was wrong with him!? I did not know what to think. I was the only Black doctor and he was white. This was obviously racism at its worst. He verbally abused me every day of every week. He would corner me when no one was around and call me racist names. I tried to avoid the interactions, but it was virtually impossible. The Medical Director ordered me to meet in his office every Friday at 5 p.m.—right before the weekend got started—to criticize my work. I repeatedly reported his racist behavior to the administration, but it was always dismissed. I endured this type of racial discrimination for one year.

———— • ————

Racism in the workplace is illegal, but it still exists in many disgraceful forms. African American workers are more likely to report that discrimination is a problem in the workplace, because they, along with other underrepresented groups, are more likely to notice microaggressions, or less overt prejudice; such as small comments, gestures, or actions.

It is a reality which many Black people feel they just have to deal with in their work environment. After reporting workplace discrimination, it is sometimes turned around and the accuser *becomes* the victimizer. Confidentiality is breeched and the identity of the accuser is revealed. There is fear of being fired after reporting racial discrimination. Retaliation often follows the reporting of discrimination. It comes in the form of alleged performance problems, which then leads to the firing of the employee. Employers frequently minimize discrimination allegations which can cause chronic stress and have a detrimental effect on one's mental and physical well-being.

———— • ————

Being the only black doctor in *a sea* of white doctors left me with feelings of isolation and loneliness. But this type of loneliness did not compare to the loneliness of losing my last parent. I received a call from my father. He expressed worry about the condition of his health. He told me he had fatigue, headaches, dizziness, chest discomfort, shortness of breath, palpitations, severe abdominal pain, profuse nausea with vomiting, and unrelenting bleeding from his rectum. He was concerned because he had lost 20 pounds over a three-week period. He thought his symptoms evolved after eating at a Chinese restaurant three weeks prior. I told my father that was probably not the cause of his health issues. Sadly, he discovered he had metastatic stomach cancer. He had approximately eight to nine months to live. I was shocked. He had not been ill. He was only in his early 70's. I felt like I was having a bad dream. Thoughts of losing my father to a terminal illness, after losing my mother to cancer, was devastating. The sadness tugged at my heart. The grief weighed on my soul. I was heartbroken and often cried myself to sleep thinking about his pain and suffering. This was my Dad. The dad who used to put me to sleep every night when I was a child. The dad who played catch with me every day after work. The dad who encouraged me to study hard in school. The dad who told me I could be anything I wanted to be. The dad who was loving and generous. The dad who ingrained in me, "The only thing society cannot take from you is your education." Being a doctor, I knew death was part of *life*, of course, but it did not make it less painful. Just like my mother, he struggled with the complications and side effects of chemotherapy. I received a call from my father. He was in the hospital. His last words to me were, "I love you son," and my last words to him were, "I love you Dad." I heard his last breath. He died in June of 2006 in Tallahassee, Florida. Dad always stressed the importance of expressing love to everyone, despite the color of their skin. That was my Dad.

———— • ————

Racism in medicine is not surprising, because medicine is part of society and society is inherently racist. Racism deems one particular group to be superior over another. The *power struggle* exists in the patient's room before the medical interaction even begins. The unnecessary distraction interferes with giving care. Racial hatred is a poison that strangles the essence of health, and until an *antidote* is developed to cure racism in medicine, strides in achieving great health for all, will continue to be stifled.

Black doctors deal with racial bias in the medical field every day. This bias might be subtle or outright overt. This can cause irreparable damage which can leave long lasting psychological and emotional scars. Black doctors are sometimes recognized as sub-standard, intellectually inept, clinically inept, and socially awkward. They are *the wrong piece in the puzzle.*

However, every day is a chance for a new beginning. A chance to erase the evilness of racism which breaks the heart of society. Every morning is an opportunity to change, to be different, and to be magnificent. We all have the choice to stay mired in the pain and suffering racism creates, or we can try to mend the broken pieces within ourselves. Racism is embedded in every nook and cranny of our society. There is no escaping it and it is seemingly here to stay. I choose, however, not to dwell on it or be offended by it. I choose to rise above the perceptions people have about me and my color. As a doctor, I concentrate on providing quality care and reflect love to all, no matter what race they are. This in turn may dispel some of the hatred in people's hearts. When all is said and done, everyone bleeds the same color, everyone suffers, and everyone needs help.

Systemic racism has no boundaries and exists despite attaining a high level of educational achievement and employment success. Being a doctor is *still* not enough, but change *is* happening—and will continue to happen—if everyone is willing to understand the reality of racism and *then* work together for a more inclusive future.

APPENDIXES

Robert and his family on their first trip to Disney World

Robert and his oldest daughter, Ashley, on her wedding day.

Robert and his sister Julie.

Robert and his wife, Nashwa on their wedding day.

Robert and his wife.

Robert performing at New York Medical College's annual Follies show.

Robert with his two daughters, Brittney (left) and Ashley (right).

Robert's Mother and Father.

*Robert's wife, Nashwa (left) and two daughters, Brittney (middle)
and Ashley (right).*

REFERENCES

Lewis, Femi. "African-American History from 1950 to 1959." ThoughtCo, Feb. 11, 2020, thoughtco.com/african-american-history-timeline-1950-1959-45442.

———— • ————

Maria Trent, Danielle G. Dooley, Jacqueline Dougé, SECTION ON ADOLESCENT HEALTH, COUNCIL ON COMMUNITY PEDIATRICS and COMMITTEE ON ADOLESCENCE. Pediatrics August 2019, 144 (2) e20191765; DOI: https://doi.org/10.1542/peds.2019-1765.

———— • ————

Lewis, Femi. "African American History Timeline: 1970 to 1979. "ThoughtCo, July19, 2020, thoughtco.com/african-american-history-timeline-1970-1979-45445.

———— • ————

Black Progress: How Far We've Come, and How Far We Have to Go. Abigail Thernstrom and Stephan Thernstrom. Sunday, March 1, 1998.

———— • ————

Krysan, M., & Moberg, S. (2016, August 25). Trends in racial attitudes. University of Illinois Institute of Government and Public Affairs. Retrieved from http://igpa.uillinois.edu/programs/racial-attitudes.

———— • ————

Understanding and Addressing Racial Disparities in Health Care. David R. Williams, Toni D. Rucker. Health Care Finance Rev. 2000 Summer; 21(4).

———— • ————

Janel Jones, John Schmitt, and Valerie Wilson, "50 Years After the Kerner Commission, African Americans Are Better Off in Many Ways, But Are Still Disadvantaged by Racial Inequality, " Economic Policy Institute, February 26, 2018".

———— • ————

The Journal of Educational Thought (JET) / Revue de la Pensée Éducative. Vol. 21, No. 3 (December 1987).

———— • ————

Cowsill, Courtney, "Stopping Racism Through Art" (2006). Pell Scholars and Senior Theses. 8. https://digitalcommons.salve.edu/pell_theses/8.

———— • ————

William Oliver PhD (2001) Cultural Racism and Structural Violence, Journal of Human Behavior in the Social Environment, 4:2-3, 1-26, DOI: 10.1300/J137v04n02_01.

———— • ————

Cite this paper as: Stephens, Darrel W., Police Discipline: A Case for Change, Washington, D.C.: U.S. Department of Justice, National Institute of Justice, 2011.

———— • ————

Nittle, Nedra Kareem. "What is the Definition of Internalized Racism?" ThoughtCo, Feb. 11, 2020, thoughtco.com/what-is-internalized-racism-2834958.

———— • ————

J Racial Ethan Health Disparities. 2017 Jun; 4(3).

———— • ————

Lewis, Femi. "African-American History Timeline: 1990 - 1999. "Thought Co, Feb. 11, 2020, thoughtco.com/african-american-history-timeline-1990-1999-45447.

———— • ————

" Racial Attitudes and Relations at the Close of the Twentieth Century. "National Research Council. 2001. America Becoming: Racial Trends and Their Consequences: Volume I. Washington, D.C.: The National Academies Press. 10.17226/9599.

———— • ————

Wikipedia, the free encyclopedia.

Made in the USA
Las Vegas, NV
29 November 2023

81828843R00057